21ST-CENTURY ECON

UNDERSTANDING TARIFFS AND TRADE BARRIERS

AVERY ELIZABETH HURT

Cavendish
Square

New York

Published in 2020 by Cavendish Square Publishing, LLC
243 5th Avenue, Suite 136, New York, NY 10016

Copyright © 2020 by Cavendish Square Publishing, LLC

First Edition

Website: cavendishsq.com

This publication represents the opinions and views of the author based on
his or her personal experience, knowledge, and research. The information
in this book serves as a general guide only. The author and publisher
have used their best efforts in preparing this book and disclaim liability
rising directly or indirectly from the use and application of this book.

All websites were available and accurate when this book was sent to press.

Library of Congress Cataloging-in-Publication Data

Names: Hurt, Avery Elizabeth, author.
Title: Understanding tariffs and trade barriers / Avery Elizabeth Hurt.
Description: First edition. | New York : Cavendish Square, 2020. |
Series: 21st-century economics | Includes bibliographical references and index.
Identifiers: LCCN 2019000923 (print) | LCCN 2019004425 (ebook) |
ISBN 9781502646125 (ebook) | ISBN 9781502646132 (library bound) |
ISBN 9781502646118 (pbk.)
Subjects: LCSH: Tariff--Juvenile literature. | Free trade--Juvenile literature. |
Protectionism--Juvenile literature.
Classification: LCC HF1713 (ebook) |
LCC HF1713 .H86 2020 (print) | DDC 382/.7--dc23
LC record available at https://lccn.loc.gov/2019000923

Editorial Director: David McNamara
Editor: Chet'la Sebree
Copy Editor: Nathan Heidelberger
Associate Art Director: Alan Sliwinski
Designer: Joe Parenteau
Production Coordinator: Karol Szymczuk
Photo Research: J8 Media

Printed in the United States of America

CONTENTS

ECONOMICS AND TRADE

Many years ago, Thomas Carlyle, a Scottish historian and writer, called economics the "dismal science." The name stuck. And it's true that economists often study gloomy subjects like poverty, job losses, and the difficulties of making sure everyone has enough to eat. On the other hand, the study of economics can help reduce the gloom in the world. Individuals as well as world leaders use economics to figure out how to increase prosperity for all people around the globe. Generally, however, economics is the scientific study of how goods and services are produced, distributed, and consumed.

Opposite: An industrial container ship arrives in port, ready to unload goods from all over the world.

Twenty-First-Century Economics

Economics is also a complicated subject. But it can be very lively and exciting, especially at times when economic theories are illustrated by what's going on in the news at the moment. The early twenty-first century provides some of those moments. During the first two decades, particularly in the late 2010s, the world's nations have had to make many important decisions about trade.

People and nations have always made deals. In the twenty-first century, the consequences of those deals have become more significant than ever before.

Those decisions can mean the difference between a thriving economy and widespread job losses. Bad trade decisions can cause companies to fail and industries to collapse. When this happens, people lose their jobs and can't feed their families. There is a lot at stake when making decisions about international trade.

The Basics of Trade

Trade seems simple enough. If you have a ham sandwich in your lunch, but you're not wild about ham, you might be willing to trade. A friend who has fried tofu cubes and is really craving a bit of meat might be happy to be your trading partner. You give him the ham, and he gives you the tofu. It's a done deal. Everyone's happy.

When you introduce money into the equation, it's slightly more complicated, but not much. You don't want your ham sandwich, but you think it's worth more than the tofu. Your friend agrees. In exchange for your sandwich, he offers to give you his tofu plus an extra twenty-five cents. You've just made a trade, even though it involved some cash. The same kind of thing happens on a much, much larger scale all around the world every day, except nations are doing the trading. They're trading all kinds of things, from the soybeans used to make your tofu to steel, automobiles, computers, and just about every kind of product you can think of.

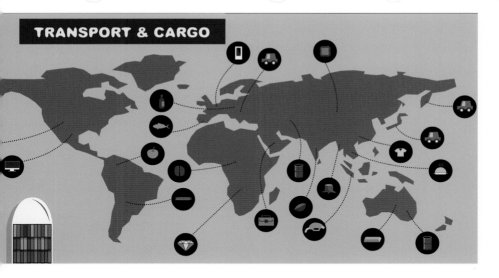

Nations around the world have a wide variety of different goods and services to trade with one another.

International Trade

Trade is very good for the world's nations (and there are almost two hundred of them). It produces jobs and creates wealth. A nation that participates in world trade is likely to have a much more vital economy and a higher standard of living than one that does not. However, in order to make the decisions that will be best for the people in their countries, world leaders often do things that limit trade. In this book, you will learn about how tariffs and other trade barriers limit trade between nations. Trade barriers are restrictions on certain types of trade. Tariffs are a type of trade barrier. Specifically, they are taxes on imported goods. Taxes are fees that the government requires a person, organization, or country to pay. In this book, you'll also see that while most economists think trade barriers are a bad idea, those barriers can sometimes be useful. You'll also learn why in the early years of the Trump administration in the United States, tariffs and trade barriers became a topic of front-page headlines.

CHAPTER 1

TARIFFS AND TRADE BARRIERS IN THE REAL WORLD

Imagine you're getting ready to buy your first car. You want something that gets good gas mileage and doesn't require a lot of maintenance. And, of course, you want a car that doesn't cost too much. So let's go shopping.

Free Trade, Choice, and Price

You look at several Honda Civics. You test drive a cute little Kia Soul. You even consider going electric with a Chevrolet Bolt. Maybe a Volkswagen Golf? All of these cars are in your price range, and all of them have features that appeal to you. Some are made by American companies,

Opposite: Japanese automobile companies, like Toyota and Honda, manufacture cars all over the world. This would not be possible without strong trade relationships.

and some are made by Asian or European companies. Even if you buy an American car, the various components of the car are made in many different places. In fact, as of 2018, the Tesla was the only car sold in the United States that was manufactured totally in the country. This means that iconic American cars such as Fords, Chevrolets, and Lincolns are partially manufactured in different countries.

What makes it possible for all these cars from all these countries to be available to you at similar prices? The answer is free trade. Free trade is an arrangement among the world's governments that allows them to trade with each other with minimal restrictions. The various companies that make these products have to compete with each other for your business. That keeps the price of goods from getting too high and keeps the wheels of commerce turning.

Free trade is good for consumers, who buy everything from groceries to school supplies to cars. It's also good for the companies who make these products. And it's good for the companies that make the raw materials used to make these products. All the companies can sell their goods in countries all around the world. This allows them to reach more customers and make more money. When they make more money, they can hire more workers and pay them well. In turn, these workers have more money to spend on products from all over the world.

Workers clock in to their jobs each day to make goods that will be sold all around the world.

Free trade has often been described as a "positive-sum" game. That basically means that when one country prospers, other countries do too. In a positive-sum game, there is enough to go around. Everyone wins.

You may have been hearing a lot about free trade in recent years, but the concept is not new. The economic theory supporting free trade has been around as long as the United States has been around.

Adam Smith Goes to a Bake Sale

In 1776, a Scottish economist named Adam Smith wrote a book called *An Inquiry into the Nature and Causes of the Wealth of Nations*. It was the first book to attempt a scientific analysis of economics. Economics students still read it today. In the book Smith writes, "In every country it always is and must be the interest of the great body of the people to buy whatever they want of those who sell it cheapest." Or, in more modern terms, it's always better for people if they can buy whatever they like for the best price they can find. This is the basic (and the oldest) argument for free trade among nations.

Smith goes on to say that the idea is so obvious that it hardly seems worth the time to defend. For the most part, in the more than two centuries since Adam Smith, economists have agreed. The reason the idea makes such good sense is that getting the best price you can for the goods you need is a key part of one of the basic principles of economics: supply and demand. The law of supply and demand is simply the relationship between how much of a product is available, how many buyers want that product, and how much that product costs. In a free market, or a market where no government regulations influence prices, supply and demand determine prices. Generally, a market is an arena or space, literal or virtual, where goods are bought and sold.

Here's an example: Imagine you are selling white chocolate macadamia nut cookies at your school bake sale. You make very good white chocolate macadamia nut cookies. Lots of people want to buy them. But you had lots of homework the night before the bake sale, so you made only two dozen cookies. Because there are far more than two dozen people waiting in line to buy your cookies, you can charge a lot for them—maybe a dollar per cookie. That price will cause some people to decide to not buy a cookie after all. This means your supply of cookies will meet the demand, which is now a bit lower because of the price increase.

However, if you raise your price too much—say you go all the way up to two dollars a cookie—many

A school bake sale is a good example of a market where goods are bought and sold according to the law of supply and demand.

of your customers will say, "Forget it. Those cookies aren't *that* good." They get out of your line, and maybe they buy some ordinary chocolate chip cookies from another kid. Suddenly your supply is greater than the demand. If you want to sell the rest of your cookies, you will need to lower the price. That will bring some customers back. The perfect price of your cookies will fall somewhere near the point where the number of cookies you have and the amount of people who want to buy them overlap.

Of course, it's not quite that simple. There are plenty of other factors involved. For example, the prices of products people must have no matter what the cost, such as medicines, don't work this way. But the point is that when trade is free, buyers and sellers work out the price that works best for everyone. The most important thing to note here is that when the market (for cookies, or anything else) is free, buyers have a lot of control over the price. If a product is not worth the price, people won't buy it. They'll go to another seller that has lower prices. That is good for cookie buyers. That's more or less what Adam Smith was talking about. It's more or less the way free markets work.

Now, we've been talking about cookies at bake sales. But of course, this applies to trade between nations as well. And that's where we get into tariffs.

How Shall I Tax Thee, Let Me Count the Ways

Free trade is a good idea most of the time. But there are reasons to occasionally put limits on trade between nations. We'll talk about those in a minute, but first let's talk about the ways trade can be limited.

One common way is by imposing tariffs. When companies have to pay taxes on imported goods, they add the cost of the tax to the cost of the product. This makes imported goods more expensive. For example, if your school charged you a tax for bringing macadamia nuts into the school, you'd have to add that cost to the price of your cookies at the bake sale. That would make it harder for you to compete with the next table selling regular, untaxed chocolate chip cookies.

If there is a tariff on cars from Germany, you'll have to pay more if you want that Volkswagen Golf you were looking at in the first part of this chapter. The American and Japanese cars will cost less because the companies selling them don't have to pay a tariff when they bring the cars into the country.

Tariffs are paid directly to the governments of the countries that have imposed tariffs. In the United States, tariffs are collected by US Customs and Border Protection. It is a part of the Department of Homeland Security.

In Canada, tariffs are paid to the Canada Border Services Agency.

In addition to tariffs, there are other trade barriers governments can impose. Companies must have licenses to import certain goods. Governments can restrict licenses if they choose. License restrictions are common with goods such as cheese and wine. Quotas are another common way of limiting trade. A quota is simply a limit

US Customs and Border Protection regulates trade but also regulates what individual citizens and visitors can bring into the United States.

on how much of a given item can be imported. Another way of controlling the amount of a certain import is for the government to declare that a given percentage of a specific product has to be made in that country.

Policies to restrict trade are generally called "protectionist" policies. This is because they are meant to protect domestic businesses—those that operate within the country itself—from foreign competition. Sometimes, as we'll soon see, there are reasons for trade barriers that aren't completely meant to be protectionist.

For Occasional Use Only

Although it's generally agreed that free trade is a good idea, there are some times and situations when trade barriers are useful. Tariffs are sometimes used to protect new industries in developing nations from competition by foreign nations that already have strong industries.

Sometimes more economically advanced nations use tariffs to protect workers in a particular industry. If that industry is facing a lot of foreign competition, domestic companies might not be able to stay in business. At the very least, they may have to lay off some workers. Placing taxes in imports makes imported goods more expensive. Domestic companies don't have to lower their prices to compete with them, as consumers will lean toward domestic products instead of expensive foreign ones.

WHO IS WTO, AND WHAT WAS GATT?

After World War II, many of the world's economies were in serious trouble. The war in Europe had left Germany in ruins. England and France weren't a whole lot better off. The United States was in much better shape, but it needed European markets for its manufactured goods. More important, it was clear that to avoid another devastating war, the world's nations needed to work together. That meant, among other things, cooperating on issues involving trade.

On January 1, 1948, twenty-three countries signed the General Agreement on Tariffs and Trade—familiarly known as GATT. This was a framework by which these countries could work together to negotiate trade rules and regulations. Over the years, GATT members met several times. The sets of negotiations were called "rounds." The main focus of the rounds was to help countries negotiate trade deals with each other to avoid tariffs and the resulting trade wars.

In 1995, GATT was replaced by the World Trade Organization (WTO). In 2019, the WTO was made up of 164 member nations. For the most part, the WTO serves the same purpose as GATT, but it is more global and concerns itself with intellectual property as well as goods. Intellectual property is the exclusive right to use or profit from an idea for an invention or from works—such as manuscripts, songs, or software programs—that a person has created. In a world that places increased value on technological innovation, the ability to control intellectual property is just as important to an economy as the ability to produce traditional goods, like wheat or steel.

The idea is that countries work together to design rules and regulations that will keep trade free and peaceful. However, not everyone loves the WTO. Some people think that the organization takes away the power of individual nations to regulate trade. Others think WTO policies favor multinational businesses over democracy and ordinary people.

In this meeting room in Geneva, Switzerland, WTO representatives from different countries meet and work out international trade deals.

This helps the domestic companies make more money. Trade barriers are also used to protect industries that are crucial to national defense.

Even when nations negotiate trade deals with each other, they leave room for some tariffs and trade restrictions on certain items.

Not a Party-Line Issue

The debate over free trade has not been keeping with the party-line politics that characterize so much debate

President Bill Clinton signed the North American Free Trade Agreement (NAFTA) in December 1993. It established trade agreements between the United States, Canada, and Mexico.

in America. Historically, Republicans have been more associated with free trade rhetoric. Democrats have tended to favor more trade restrictions because of their support for industrial workers, small farmers, and labor unions. However, in the early twenty-first century, the world economy has grown more interconnected. For that reason, people from both parties have been increasingly in favor of creating trade barriers, including Republicans like Donald Trump.

The history of free trade has been colorful. Not long after Adam Smith wrote that the benefits of free trade were almost too obvious to need explanation, Alexander Hamilton explained why a little protectionism under the right circumstances might be a good idea.

CHAPTER 2

TARIFFS IN HISTORY

Tariffs and protectionism go back a long way in history. They've been around ever since there have been nation-states to trade with each other. The practice of imposing barriers to trade was part of what led to the American Revolution. People have been arguing the pros and cons of protectionism ever since.

No Taxation without Representation

By the eighteenth century, European nations had started to base their economic systems on competition with each other. They passed numerous laws to regulate trade, both imports and exports, and imposed high tariffs. This often resulted in devastating wars. These were not trade wars but real wars with guns and cannons, such as the Opium

Opposite: American colonists made clear their opposition to taxes on imported goods by dumping cases of tea into Boston Harbor in the late eighteenth century.

Wars between Britain and China and the Anglo-Dutch War. One of the most famous wars of the eighteenth century was also ignited by trade disputes. And this one resulted in a new nation.

The phrase "no taxation without representation" was the rallying cry that led to the American Revolution. The taxes that angered the colonists were tariffs. Britain placed tariffs (also called "import duties") on many of the goods that the colonists needed but had to buy from Britain. The Townshend Acts, implemented by the British in 1767, were particularly troublesome to the colonists. They added tariffs to many important goods, such as glass, paper, paint, and tea. The tax on tea especially infuriated the colonists, who drank enormous amounts of tea. The duties imposed by the Townshend Acts weren't protectionist. They were intended, in part, to raise money to pay the salaries of colonial governors and judges so that these leaders would be loyal to the British government instead of the colonists. They were a powerful economic tool for controlling the colonies. It didn't work, of course. These tariffs were so unpopular that they convinced the colonists to rebel against Britain and establish the United States.

The United States Constitution was ratified, or made official, in 1788. One of the first things the new Congress did was to pass the Tariff Act of 1789. It placed at least a 5 percent tax on many foreign goods.

Alexander Hamilton was America's first secretary of the Treasury. It was his job to get the new nation's financial system up and running. When the United States was young, it was mostly an agricultural nation. The United States sold tobacco, rice, and some cotton to European nations.

Alexander Hamilton was the first secretary of the Treasury of the United States. He was also an early American supporter of tariffs.

In turn, the United States bought manufactured goods from Europe. Hamilton believed that in order to remain independent from Britain and other European countries, the United States would have to have factories as well as farms. He also wanted the United States to be able to compete as an equal in world markets. In order to do this, the country would need to have manufactured goods to sell.

Hamilton agreed with Adam Smith that free trade was a good idea. He opposed high, protectionist tariffs. However, he did think that temporarily adding modest tariffs to imports from England and other European nations was necessary to jump-start manufacturing in the United States. These tariffs would make imported goods cost more than the same goods bought from an American company. This would encourage American companies to produce more products. In turn, this would encourage Americans to buy the locally produced products rather than the imported ones.

Hamilton had another reason for supporting tariffs. The new country was broke and had a huge amount of debt left over from the American Revolution. Taxing imports would help it raise much-needed money.

Different Leaders, Different Policies

Hamilton's tariff policies weren't exactly protectionist, but they were controversial, even then. Thomas Jefferson favored an agricultural society and wasn't eager to develop industry. He also wanted to keep the central government small, leaving more of the power and money in the hands of state governments. Jefferson also had another reason for opposing these tariffs. He believed that tariffs would hurt the farmers who sold their crops in Europe. If the United States placed tariffs on goods it imported from other countries, those countries could in turn place tariffs on goods the United States exported to them. This would make American tobacco, rice, cotton, and so on more expensive in Europe. This would make it harder for American farmers to sell their crops. Hamilton's plan would help industry but harm farmers.

However, even Jefferson came around to the idea. He realized that if the young nation didn't want to be dependent on other countries, it had to develop the industries that would provide Americans the materials and products they needed.

In 1816, under President James Madison, Congress passed tariffs that were unquestionably protectionist. The Tariff of 1816 raised taxes on imports into the 25–30 percent range. In 1828, these rates were raised to around 50 percent on average. After that, tariffs trended back downward for many years, reaching a low point in 1857. Later in the nineteenth century, American industries began to demand protection from what they called "cheap labor" in Europe. Protectionist policies again became very popular. Those policies seemed to be effective, too. US industries thrived, particularly oil and steel. Indeed, US Steel became the first billion-dollar company in the United States in 1901. However, most economists now think that the boost in industry was not due primarily to protectionism.

In 1913, under President Woodrow Wilson, Congress again lowered tariffs to reasonable levels. The economy continued to do well until the Great Depression. This was a devastating economic slowdown. It began in the United States in 1929 but quickly spread to the rest of

On many occasions throughout US history, the steel giant US Steel has benefited from tariffs and other protectionist policies.

the world. In the early days of this depression, the US Congress passed the infamous Smoot-Hawley Tariff Act with the goal of helping US businesses get through the economic downturn. US tariffs were already high. Smoot-Hawley jacked them up even higher. US trading partners responded with tariffs of their own aimed at the United States. These policies made the worldwide depression much worse. The damage done by the Smoot-Hawley tariffs and similar tariffs convinced almost everyone of the wisdom of free trade.

Modern Trade Policies

As the global economy became ever more interconnected in the years after World War II, the commitment to free trade was only reinforced. It became clear that if American companies were going to succeed in the global economy, freer trade policies were essential. The public supported free trade as well, having often paid more for essential goods when they were the victims of tariffs. In the years after World War II, the United States began to negotiate trading agreements with other nations. This allowed countries to work out deals that protected their interests without getting into dangerous trade competitions with each other.

By the end of the twentieth century, most large businesses were international. Trade agreements worked better for them than protectionist policies. Businesses began to throw their support behind these agreements. However, in an interesting shift, many people began to oppose free trade because it was seen as enriching the wealthy at the expense of the poor, the middle class, and the environment. Many modern leaders, even Democrats Bill Clinton and Barack Obama, argued that free, global trade is a good thing in the long run. They pointed out that it lifts more people out of poverty worldwide. They also believed that it gives the United States greater bargaining power when it comes to a wide range of issues, including environmental ones such as climate agreements.

Not long after he became president in 2017, Donald Trump imposed a wide range of tariffs on goods from many nations, including some of the United States' closest allies. For instance, he placed tariffs on steel imports. His reasoning for this was twofold. First, he argued that in case of war, the United States would not be able to produce enough of its own weapons and vehicles if it did not make more of its own steel. Most of the steel the US buys comes from long-time solid allies, particularly Canada. Nonetheless, that is a common argument in support of tariffs. Trump was not the first to make it. His second argument was that taxing steel imports would encourage US manufacturers to buy US steel. This would, in turn, increase the profits of American steel companies and create more jobs for Americans in the steel industry.

During his campaign rallies, Donald Trump promised to impose tariffs on goods from China. He was elected president in 2016 and kept that promise.

Allies weren't the only targets of Trump's protectionism. He also hit China with enormous tariffs on a wide range of products. In 2019, the United States had a trade deficit with China. This simply means that the US imported more goods from China than it exported to China. The tariffs on Chinese goods were meant to reduce this deficit. In addition, Trump said these tariffs were meant to punish China for various unfair economic practices, such as theft of intellectual property.

These countries, allies and rivals alike, responded with tariffs of their own, creating what is called a trade war. Trump reassured a nervous public that trade wars are "easy to win." History, however, suggests otherwise.

ABOMINATION!

A dispute over tariffs nearly caused a civil war in the United States almost three decades before the US Civil War started. The problem began in 1828 when the US government placed high tariffs on manufactured goods.

The tariffs aided the textile industry in the Northeast but stood to harm the economies of the agricultural Southern states. These states depended on selling cotton to the British textile industry. Southern politicians were livid. In 1832, President Andrew Jackson softened the tariffs, but not enough. Southern politicians were so upset that they called this the "tariff of abominations," meaning it was worthy of hatred and disgust.

Many South Carolina politicians were calling for South Carolina to secede from the Union over this issue. Instead, John C. Calhoun, who was Jackson's vice president and was from South Carolina, invoked the nullification doctrine. This was a legal principle originally supported by James Madison and Thomas Jefferson. It basically meant that when states believed a policy of the federal government had exceeded the government's authority, they had the right to declare that policy null and void in their states. And that's exactly what South Carolina

John C. Calhoun, the seventh vice president of the United States, was a staunch defender of the political rights of the Southern states and of slavery.

did. Andrew Jackson was having none of it. He asked Congress to pass a law that allowed him to use federal troops to enforce the law. Congress stepped in and worked out a compromise with South Carolina. This averted an armed conflict.

South Carolina saved face this time, but the incident only added to the South's perception that it was being disadvantaged by Northern states. In 1860, South Carolina finally did secede, over slavery this time, beginning the US Civil War.

CHAPTER 3

TARIFFS AND TRADE WARS: A DANGEROUS SPIRAL

In the past, disputes about tariffs have led to very real wars. Most of the time, however, they lead to trade wars. In trade wars, no guns are fired and no bombs are dropped. But the damage to economies, businesses, and even individuals and families can be severe.

Win Some, Lose Some

In 2002, the US steel industry was in trouble. In an attempt to save the jobs of people working in the industry, President George W. Bush placed tariffs on steel. The move backfired terribly. In addition to alienating trading

Opposite: The US steel industry isn't the only one affected by tariffs. These Welsh steelworkers worry about the effect UK politics and international trade relations will have on their jobs.

partners, the tariffs cost more jobs than they saved. Companies that sold steel made more money because they didn't have to lower their prices to compete with imports. Meanwhile, however, companies that bought steel had to pay more for that steel, making it more difficult for them to make a profit. It turned out that there were far more people working in industries that bought steel than working in industries that produced it. These were industries that made things from large appliances to small steel-containing parts for equipment and vehicles. Industrial construction firms were hit hard by these tariffs, too. Most of these companies were small, with fewer than five hundred employees.

So while the tariffs may have helped a few big steel companies, they hurt far more people than they helped. More than two hundred thousand Americans lost their jobs in 2002 because of these tariffs. That amounted to more people than worked in the entire steel industry. This is often the case with tariffs. They may help one industry, temporarily, but generally they hurt many others. It can be difficult to predict how deep and lasting damage from tariffs will be.

The 2002 steel tariffs could have been much worse than they were. Almost as soon as they were implemented, the Bush administration began granting exceptions to various imports. Also, the tariffs didn't last long. Bush removed the tariffs after the World Trade Organization ruled that they violated global trade rules.

A Downward Spiral

Protectionism can backfire in other ways as well. For instance, tariffs contributed to the impact of the Great Depression. Trade wars can sometimes lead to recessions as well. A recession is an economic slowdown that is not as severe as a depression but is still hard on an economy and its citizens. During recessions, people find it harder to get jobs. Since more people are looking for jobs, companies can offer lower pay and skimpier benefits to workers than they do during times of full employment.

When governments start hitting each other with tariffs, customers must pay higher prices for the things they buy. When goods become more expensive, people buy fewer of them. When companies don't have enough buyers for their products, they can't afford to pay as many employees. This means they have to let some workers go. They also might cut the wages or hours worked for the employees they keep. The increased unemployment and lower income cause people to spend less money, which makes the situation worse for companies and the economy. It creates a downward spiral.

Trade wars can end up affecting many different industries. For example, when the US placed tariffs on

This Canadian shopper is less likely to buy products imported from the United States if tariffs have made them more expensive.

Canadian steel in 2018, Canada responded with tariffs on dozens of imports from the United States, including orange juice, yogurt, peanut butter, whiskey, chocolate, and a variety of metals. What started with the steel industry ended up affecting many others. These situations can have complex effects that spread throughout a nation's economy. People who have nothing to do with the industry the tariffs were designed to protect can get hurt.

This doesn't happen in just one country. All the countries involved in trade wars risk falling into recessions. People all over the world buy goods from each other. Now that the world's economies are so interdependent, when one major economy starts using tariffs, everyone feels the effects.

Changing with the Times

Another way tariffs can backfire is by trapping workers in a dying industry. Politicians often use tariffs to try to support industries that are in trouble, as Bush did with steel in 2002 and Trump in 2018. But not only can this cause short-term problems for workers, it can cause long-term problems as well. Trump's tariffs on Chinese goods were intended to repair America's trade deficit with China. One of the reasons for that deficit is that the United States is rapidly moving from a manufacturing-based economy to a service-based economy. Service industries include finance, information technology, software, health care, education, and media. The United States may not export as many manufactured goods as it once did, but it exports plenty of services. Even the services it doesn't export are key to the nation's economic well-being. There are jobs in these industries for people who are trained for them.

These adult learners are mastering new skills so that they will be able to find jobs in the changing economy.

Change can be upsetting and disruptive, but it is not necessarily a bad thing. The shift in emphasis from manufacturing to the service industry has driven economic growth in the United States, but it has led to job losses for manufacturing workers. Protectionist policies that try to prop up dying industries reduce the incentive to retrain employees so that they can get better-paying jobs in other industries. Tariffs may help save manufacturing jobs in the short term, but in the long term, these workers might be worse off for not having adapted to a service-based economy.

Not Always a Bad Idea

Despite all the things that can go wrong when a country embraces protectionist policies, tariffs can have some benefits. Tariffs are essentially taxes. Tariffs are paid to the government, so the government gets more revenue, or income, from them. This was one of the reasons for tariffs in the early days of the United States. The country was broke and in debt and desperately needed cash.

Some businesses can benefit, too, in the short run. When imported goods cost more, local companies make more sales. Cutting out competition from imports can temporarily boost sales for the targeted industries. Some workers may benefit as well, at least for a time. When companies get more business, they can afford to hire new employees or raise the pay of the ones they already have.

If the tariffs are not too long-lived or widespread, then they can do some good. Small tariffs can allow nations to aid an industry here and there without risking

American autoworkers gathered on Capitol Hill in July 2018 to protest proposed steel tariffs that could cost them their jobs.

a trade war and other dangerous consequences of protectionist policies.

Although they are risky, protectionist policies have always been surprisingly popular. Politicians often support protectionist policies because they go over well with some voters. Large companies who benefit from tariffs often have a great deal of political power. They can afford to spend lots of money supporting candidates who promise tariffs that will help their industries. Individuals, however, are the ones who have to pay more or less for the things they must buy.

They can be swayed by campaign promises supporting US businesses and industries as well. The jobs that are saved by protectionism are often concentrated in one industry—steel production, for example. It's easy to see that benefit. The jobs that are lost are scattered across many sectors of the economy. It may be harder to connect them directly to a tariff imposed on a seemingly unrelated industry. The benefits of protectionism show up quickly. The negative effects take a little longer to arrive. That's why it's not always clear when the costs of these policies outweigh the benefits.

QUICK Q&A

If tariffs are a tax on imported goods, how does that help domestic companies trying to sell their goods in the domestic market?

Imported goods will be more expensive to buy because of the additional tax. That means domestic companies can charge a lower price for the same products, making it easier for them to sell their goods.

What happens to the money collected by the government from tariffs?

In the United States, the money collected from tariffs goes directly to the United States Treasury and becomes a part of the federal budget. In Canada, these taxes also go directly to the federal budget. Canada uses these taxes to help workers who have been harmed by the trade war.

Who makes decisions about exemptions to tariffs?

In the United States, requests for exemptions are decided by the US Department of Commerce. Other nations have similar agencies that make these decisions.

In the United States, does Congress play a role in imposing or preventing tariffs?

The US Constitution gave Congress the responsibility of regulating trade. However, after World War I, Congress gradually passed laws that gave the president more power to make decisions about trade. These laws allow the president to impose tariffs or quotas when the security of the country is at risk or when other countries engage in unfair trading practices. Congress still has to approve trade agreements, however.

CHAPTER 4

THE UNITED STATES STARTS A MODERN TRADE WAR

Trade wars rarely have good outcomes for any of the parties involved. That does not, however, prevent leaders from starting them.

Going Toe to Toe with China

In June 2018, President Donald Trump imposed tariffs on a wide range of goods from China. China responded by imposing their own stiff tariffs on US products such as vehicles, crude oil, and pork.

This kind of "you hit me/I hit you" trade battle can be done with surgical precision. The Chinese seemed to have carefully chosen to place tariffs on products, such as pork,

In November 2017, Chinese leader Xi Jinping hosted President Donald Trump in Beijing. Among other things, the two men discussed their nations' trading relationship.

that came from areas of the United States that had voted for Trump in the 2016 election. Trump's electoral victory had depended on votes from key states. The Chinese made it clear that they were willing to specifically target those states to impact Trump's chances at reelection. This was personal. Soon, however, the trade war escalated. The Chinese retaliated with tariffs on virtually all US imports.

Both economies were quite strong at this time, so they were expected to be able to weather some damage from the trade war. China had a few other advantages as well. In a trade war with the United States, China couldn't play tit-for-tat long because they imported far fewer US goods than the United States imported Chinese goods. But China had other options. They could have made their tariffs even higher. They could have added import quotas on US goods, creating a different kind of trade barrier. They could have restricted travel to China by US citizens. They could have shielded Chinese companies that were harmed by the tariffs by cutting their taxes.

China could have also fought on another front. The Chinese government controls its central bank and can easily lower the value of its currency, the yuan. Devaluing the yuan relative to the dollar would make Chinese exports cheaper for Americans to buy. This would have taken some of the sting out of the tariffs, blunting their effect. It would have also made US goods more expensive for Chinese consumers to buy, strengthening the effect of China's tariffs. This could have turned a trade war into a currency war, creating even more global economic problems.

On Main Street

After the first round of tariffs went into effect, it didn't take long for businesses to cry foul. In September of 2018, shortly after the trade war with China had begun, several companies announced that the tariffs were hurting their profits. Energy and technology companies were among the first to complain. Other industries soon followed. Later that autumn, Ford Motor Company announced that tariffs on steel and aluminum were costing them over $1 billion. This would no doubt lead to higher automobile prices across the industry, Ford said.

In September 2018, just before the first round of tariffs took effect, Walmart wrote a letter to the Trump administration asking them to reconsider the tariffs. The giant retailer explained how painful these tariffs would be to their customers, particularly for low-income families. In the letter, Walmart explained to the president that no matter how retailers dealt with the new taxes, the results would be bad for average Americans. The White House ignored their pleas, and consumers soon felt the pain in their shopping carts. Walmart and Target announced that prices for a wide range of consumer goods would

In 2018, tariffs affected the US auto industry. In September, Ford CEO Jim Hackett warned that the trade war could cost the company $1 billion.

go up in the wake of the tariffs. Prices increased for school supplies, shampoo, deodorant, baseball gloves, bicycles, tuna, hammers, and appliances, to name only a few. The list was long.

On Wall Street

The tariffs also troubled the stock market. By the end of 2018, the US stock market was reacting wildly to any blip in the trade war. Historically, the stock market hasn't responded well to tariffs. Healthy trade is essential to a healthy stock market. A trade war signals that an economic slowdown might be just ahead. This makes investors less willing to invest in American businesses by buying stocks. They are afraid that the stocks will lose value when the economy slows down and that they'll lose money. If it looks like the economy is about to take a serious downturn, investors will start selling off the stock they already own before it loses value. This can cause many others to sell, making the value of most stocks go down. When this happens, businesses and people who invest in businesses lose a lot of money. Ordinary people don't feel it at first, but it can have a powerful effect on them in time. When businesses lose money, they hire fewer people and pay them less.

In addition, the trade war with China seemed to have only increased one of the problems it was meant to solve: the trade deficit. In 2018, the United States trade deficit with China actually increased by 7 percent over what it had been the year before. One reason for this was a surge in exports of products from China, such as soybeans, that were expected to be hit hard by the tariffs. Chinese soybean producers wanted to get as much of their product shipped and sold before the tariffs took effect or before they escalated too much.

The effects weren't felt just in the US and China. This trade war had global effects as well. Trade growth around the world began to slow down, and so did foreign investment. Trade wars are always a drag on the

NOT MY JOB!

Tariffs often seem like a good idea in theory or in the heat of a political campaign. But when the effects start to show up in the towns, factories, and lives of individuals, things aren't always so clear-cut. And sometimes they are very clear-cut, but in a bad way.

In 2018, a steel mill in Pennsylvania began to feel the effects of the steel tariffs. The Russian-owned mill,

Many businesses have been boarded up in Farrell, Pennsylvania, since the steel industry went into decline. Tariffs have only made matters worse.

NLMK Pennsylvania, is located in Farrell, Pennsylvania. It buys raw steel from Russia and turns it into coils before selling it to other companies. Those companies use the steel coils to manufacture pipes or automobiles. Tariffs on imported steel meant that the company was having to pay more for their raw materials. They were having trouble staying afloat. Workers were worried that they would lose their jobs. And, in Farrell, Pennsylvania, there weren't many more jobs to get.

Reporters from National Public Radio visited the town in June of 2018. They discovered that many of the steelworkers there actually supported the idea of tariffs. They just hoped that their company would get an exception to the tax. The town's city manager, however, said that the tariffs were "an abomination" for his community. After many years of losing jobs as steel mills closed, Farrell had finally found some hope when NLKM opened there. However, the very tariffs they hoped would save their industry could have ended up costing them their jobs.

economies of the countries involved. But, in the twenty-first century, the world's economies are so intertwined that it is impossible for a trade war between two large nations to not have a powerful effect on other nations.

However, in the long term, the US-China trade war may ultimately be found to have helped other nations in some ways. China could buy from other nations some of the products and materials it once imported from the United States. When it comes to exporting its goods—particularly things like laptop computers and cell phones—China has plenty of other customers. For instance, India as well as African and Latin American countries are some of the best markets for Chinese goods these days.

We Have a Deal. Not!

In December 2018, world leaders met in Buenos Aires, Argentina, for the annual meeting of the G20. The G20 is a group of the world's twenty leading economies. At the December 2018 meeting, Trump talked with President Xi Jinping of China. Trump emerged from the meeting claiming victory. The two had agreed, said Trump, to a ninety-day truce in the trade war. During that time, the two parties would negotiate an agreement. The effects of this truce were seen fairly quickly. During the month of December, China not only cut tariffs on more than seven hundred US imports but also imported over

The stock market is extremely responsive to the ups and downs of trade wars. Good news can make it surge; bad news can make it plummet.

1.5 million tons (1.36 million metric tons) of soybeans from the United States. The stock market reacted joyously.

Despite the boost in the stock market, tensions continued between the two countries during this three-month period as talks continued. The March 1, 2019, deadline of the ninety-day truce came and went without any resolution. However, at the time, both countries were hopeful a compromise could be reached.

Tariffs can cause a lot of economic distress. However, they can be quickly reversed. This may be why politicians often use them to appease certain groups—such as steelworkers—and threaten other countries. Then, they can withdraw or soften tariffs before the damage becomes too widespread. As of this writing, it was not known how long the US trade dispute with China would last, or what its long-term effects would be.

CHAPTER 5

ECONOMISTS HAVE THEIR SAY

Economics is a tricky science, and experts in the field often do not see eye to eye about economic policies. In fact, there are jokes about it. One popular joke goes like this: "What happens when you put ten economists in a room? You get eleven opinions." However, while experts are happy to debate each other about a variety of economic topics, when it comes to tariffs and other protectionist policies, there is not much disagreement among economists.

Dear Mr. President

In May 2018, President Donald Trump received a letter strongly advising him to abandon his protectionist policies.

Opposite: World-renowned economists that come from strong programs like the one at the University of Chicago, pictured here, often disagree. However, many agree about the dangers of tariffs.

It was signed by more than one thousand economists. Fifteen of them had previously won the Nobel Prize in Economics. These experts came from all over the political and geographic map. Those signing the letter included advisors to former presidents both Republican and Democratic. They consisted of professors from Ivy League universities as well as state universities. All parts of the nation were represented from the Northeast to the Southeast and across the nation's heartland to the West Coast.

The letter stated that protectionist policies threatened the global economy. They reminded the president of the dire consequences of the Smoot-Hawley tariffs in the 1930s. A similar letter, signed by a similar number of economists, had been sent to President Herbert Hoover in 1930 to try to persuade him to abandon the Smoot-Hawley tariffs. Those tariffs, the new letter explained, had harmed many Americans. The economists warned President Trump not to make the same mistake. "Congress did not take economists' advice in 1930, and Americans across the country paid the price," they wrote.

The letter went on to point out that the principles of economics had not changed since 1930, but the world had. Those changes made tariffs even more unwise in 2018 than they had been ninety years before. In 2018, the world's economies were more dependent on free trade than they ever had been. The letter then summed up the view of the world's economists by quoting the 1930 letter: "We are convinced that increased protective duties would be a mistake. They would operate, in general, to increase the prices which domestic consumers would have to pay. A higher level of protection would raise the cost of living and injure the great majority of our citizens."

Many Voices

American Paul Samuelson was one of the most influential economists of the twentieth century. He was an advocate of free trade, yet he acknowledged that importing lower-priced goods from nations with developing economies could hurt American producers. His solution was not protectionism, which he said would only do more harm. Instead, he advocated increasing trade and increased productivity, which would raise the average standard of living enough to raise all boats.

In his 2017 book *Clashing over Commerce: A History of US Trade Policy*, American economist Douglas A. Irwin argues that protectionist policies in the decades after the Civil War were not the reason for the nation's industrial growth during that period. Instead, Irwin says, the industrial boom was due in large part to the high rate of immigration during that period. This created a large labor force and increased productivity. On the other hand,

Irwin thinks that the effect of the Smoot-Hawley tariffs on the Great Depression has been overblown. He says they were definitely harmful but probably didn't increase the severity of the Depression as much as others say.

While virtually all economists agree that protectionism is a poor idea, not everyone thinks it is a guaranteed disaster. Economist Paul Krugman points out that while trade wars are bad, they aren't necessarily catastrophic. Particularly in times of high productivity, the damage from

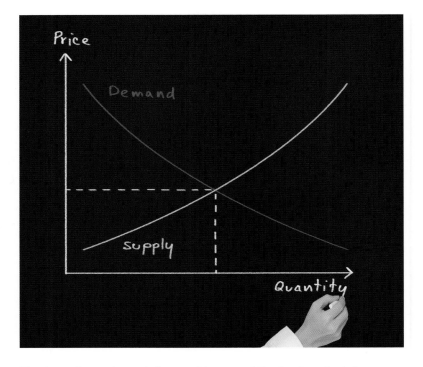

The law of supply and demand is one of the basic principles of the science of economics. If demand for Chinese goods decreases, so, too, will prices—and hopefully tariffs as well.

tariffs might not be deep enough to cause long-lasting harm. However, it is important, he says, that trade wars be kept relatively short.

During the US trade dispute with China, Robert Scott, director of trade research at the Economic Policy Institute, said that tariffs on Chinese steel could work if they were used in a coordinated way among several nations. He also argued that fears of a trade war were overblown, since China has historically been more dependent on the United States than the United States has been on China. However, Scott pointed out the need for a careful strategy behind the tariffs. Such planning, he said, would need to be managed from a global perspective, not just from the perspective of one country against another.

Peace on Earth

Many economists and historians point out that free trade is good not just for the global economy but for the peace and stability of the world. Trade wars are generally not physically violent (though they have led to terrible wars). However, they can and do increase hostilities between nations. They also create an "us versus them" attitude that can cause the peoples of various nations to feel hostile toward each other.

An interdependent world makes war riskier for nations. If your economy is tied to another by trade, it's

A FEW MORE FACTS

- Tariffs are taxes on imports. But you won't find US taxes on the United States' exports. Why not? Because Article I, Section 9 of the US Constitution forbids it: "No Tax or Duty shall be laid on Articles exported from any State."

- One reason the outcome of tariffs is so hard to predict is that imports and exports are intertwined. US manufacturing relies on imports to produce the goods it exports. According to data from George Mason University, imports contribute 15.3 percent of the value of US exports.

- Average tariffs in the United States fell from nearly 60 percent in 1932 to under 5 percent in 2018. Though there were occasional tariff spikes during this period, the trend has been consistently downward.

- In 1927, the League of Nations organized the first World Economic Conference to help iron out trade agreements between nations. However, the Great Depression caused a new wave of protectionism. This, in part, led to nationalism, an extreme form of patriotism, and other conditions that contributed to the outbreak of World War II.
- The European Union began as a trading partnership among European nations. The intent was to ensure prosperity for all EU members and reduce the chances of conflicts among European countries.
- Being able to trade with other nations on a more or less equal footing is one of the most important factors in lifting developing nations out of poverty.
- Nations with strong economies, like the United States, have an advantage in trade wars.

This street fair in New York features individuals from many nations buying and selling goods. This is possible when international relations are healthy and strong.

not a great idea to go to war with that nation. But that's not the only reason free trade contributes to a more peaceful world. Daniel Griswold, a trade expert at George Mason University, has pointed out that trade increases communication between the world's peoples. That, in turn, reduces the suspicion and hatred that leads to wars.

In the letter sent to Presidents Hoover and Trump, the world's greatest economists wrote, "We would urge our Government to consider the bitterness which a policy of higher tariffs would inevitably inject into our international relations. A tariff war does not furnish good soil for the growth of world peace."

Almost everyone agrees that unfair trade practices need to be addressed. Most people, however, favor doing this by negotiation rather than by starting trade wars. The reasons go beyond the fact that trade wars rarely end well for anyone. They have to do with the nature of the global economy and the need for nations to work peaceably together to bring economic stability to all people.

GLOSSARY

abomination An act or object that is seen to be worthy of extreme hatred or disgust.

consumer An individual who buys goods or services.

currency The basic unit of money used in a particular country or region, e.g., the dollar, the pound, and the euro.

depression A long and severe decline in economic activity, usually characterized by high unemployment.

doctrine A principle or policy.

domestic Existing within a particular nation as opposed to outside of it; the opposite of foreign.

economics The scientific study of how goods and services are produced, distributed, and consumed.

export To send domestic-made products to other countries.

import To bring foreign-made products into a country.

intellectual property Works, such as manuscripts, music, or software, or inventions created by a person for which that person has the exclusive rights.

market The area or space (literal or virtual) where goods are bought and sold.

nationalism An extreme form of patriotism that elevates one country's culture and policies over those of all other countries or peoples.

protectionism Policies such as tariffs and other trade barriers that are aimed at defending a country's industries against foreign competition.

quota A set amount of a particular item.

recession A temporary setback in economic activity, including manufacturing and trade, often leading to unemployment and lower wages.

revenue Income of a government, organization, or business.

sector A branch or division of a nation's economy.

stocks A portion of the value of a publicly traded company.

supply and demand This economic principle explores the balance between the amount of a good or service available (supply) and the desire of consumers to buy it (demand); this balance is affected by the price of the goods or services available and buyers' willingness to pay that price.

tariff A tax a country imposes on goods imported from another country.

tax A fee paid to a government.

trade barrier A government-instituted restriction on international trade, like a tariff or a quota.

trade deficit A situation where a country buys (imports) more products from another country than it sells (exports) to that country.

FURTHER INFORMATION

Books

Cooke, Tim. *Money and Trade*. What's the Big Idea? New York: Cavendish Square Publishing, 2018.

Hollander, Barbara Gottfried. *Understanding Economics: Trade and Exchange*. New York: Rosen, 2019.

Lusted, Marcia Amidon. *Understanding Economics: Supply and Demand*. New York: Rosen, 2019.

Munsey, Lizzie, and Kate Johnson, eds. *The Economics Book: Big Ideas Simply Explained*. New York: Dorling Kindersley, 2012.

Uhl, Xina M. *The Economics of Global Trade*. Understanding Global Trade & Commerce. Philadelphia: Mason Crest, 2017.

Websites

Bizkids

http://www.bizkids.com

This entertaining and engaging site teaches middle grade and high school students about money and finance.

Investopedia

https://www.investopedia.com

This website covers basic economic concepts in an accessible way. It provides quizzes and useful links.

Videos

Global Trade

https://www.youtube.com/watch?v=E8GxX9uTEng

This video gives a quick but thorough overview of international trade.

How Tariffs Work: International Economics

https://www.youtube.com/watch?v=HWFV-bYfm_4

This video uses example and graphs to explain tariffs and trade barriers.

Organizations

American Economic Association

2014 Broadway Suite 305
Nashville, TN 37203
(615) 322-2595
Website: https://www.aeaweb.org

The AEA is an organization dedicated to supporting economic research and education. It takes no partisan positions on the issues it covers.

Canadian Economics Association

University of British Columbia
2053 Main Mall
Vancouver, BC V6T 1Z2
Canada
(613) 454-5275
Website: https://economics.ca/en/index.php

This organization is dedicated to advancing economic education through study and research.

Global Affairs Canada

125 Sussex Drive
Ottawa, ON K1A 0G2
Canada
(613) 944-4000
Website: https://www.international.gc.ca/gac-amc/index.aspx?lang=eng

This organization manages Canada's diplomatic relations and promotes international trade.

Law and Economics Center of George Mason University, Antonin Scalia Law School

3301 Fairfax Drive
Hazel Hall, Suite 440
Arlington, VA 22201
(703) 993-8040
Website: https://masonlec.org

The LEC is a leading academic center for the study and research of economics and law. Many of its articles and educational pieces are accessible for non-experts.

National Constitution Center
Independence Mall
525 Arch Street
Philadelphia, PA 19106
(215) 409-6600
Website: https://www.constitutioncenter.org

An institution established by the US Congress to spread information about the US Constitution, this organization provides information and learning activities related to the US government.

World Trade Organization
Centre William Rappard
Rue de Lausanne, 154
1211 Geneva
Switzerland
Email: enquiries@wto.org
Website: https://www.wto.org

The World Trade Organization deals with the rules of trade among nations. It is an organization of world governments that works to ensure that trade flows smoothly and as freely as possible between nations.

SELECTED BIBLIOGRAPHY

Campbell, Alexia Fernández. "Trump's Protectionist Economic Plan Is Nothing New." *Atlantic*, January 9, 2017. https://www.theatlantic.com/business/archive/2017/01/trumps-protectionist-economic-plan-is-nothing-new/512585.

Carden, Art. "1,100+ Economists: No Trump Tariffs." *Forbes*, May 4, 2018. https://www.forbes.com/sites/artcarden/2018/05/04/1100-economists-no-trump-tariffs/#ebb5d7040fba.

Destler, I. M. "America's Uneasy History with Free Trade." *Harvard Business Review*, April 28, 2016. https://hbr.org/2016/04/americas-uneasy-history-with-free-trade.

Francois, Joseph, and Laura M. Baughman. "The Unintended Consequences of US Steel Import Tariffs: A Quantification of the Impact During 2002." Trade Partnership Worldwide, February 4, 2003. http://www.tradepartnership.com/pdf_files/2002jobstudy.pdf.

Frieden, Jeffry A. *Global Capitalism: It's Fall and Rise in the Twentieth Century*. New York: Norton, 2006.

Gallarotti, Giulio. "Trump's Protectionism Continues Long History of US Rejection of Free Trade." *Conversation*, February 21, 2018. https://theconversation.com/trumps-protectionism-continues-long-history-of-us-rejection-of-free-trade-91190.

Gardner, Sarah. "From Alexander Hamilton to Trump, the US Has a Long History of America-First Policies." *Marketplace*, August 11, 2017. https://www.marketplace.org/2017/08/11/world/trade-stories-globalization-and-backlash/why-american-protectionism-still-rings.

Griswold, Daniel. "Peace on Earth, Free Trade for Men." Cato Institute, December 31, 1998. https://www.cato.org/publications/commentary/peace-earth-free-trade-men.

Hamilton, Alexander. "Report on Manufactures." National Archives: Founders Online, December 5, 1791. https://founders.archives.gov/documents/Hamilton/01-10-02-0001-0007.

Irwin, Douglas A. *Clashing over Commerce: A History of US Trade Policy*. Chicago, IL: University of Chicago Press, 2017.

Krugman, Paul R. "Is Free Trade Passe?" *Journal of Economic Perspectives* 1, no. 2 (Fall 1987): 131–144. https://www.aeaweb.org/articles?id=10.1257/jep.1.2.131.

Long, Heather. "There Are 'Nuggets of Truth' to What Trump Says About Trade." *Washington Post*, June 8, 2018. https://www.washingtonpost.com/news/wonk/wp/2018/06/08/there-are-nuggets-of-truth-to-what-trump-says-about-trade/?utm_term=.c9383c01608a.

"Open Letter to President Trump and Congress." National Taxpayers Union, May 3, 2018. https://www.ntu.org/library/doclib/Embargoed-Economists-Letter-2018-1.pdf.

Smith, Adam. *Wealth of Nations Book I-III*. New York: Penguin, 1986.

Ulrich, Lana. "Donald Trump and the History of Trade and Tariffs." National Constitution Center, January 18, 2017. https://constitutioncenter.org/blog/donald-trump-and-the-history-of-tariffs-and-trade.

Wolman, Paul. *Most Favored Nation: The Republican Revisionists and US Tariff Policy, 1897–1912*. Chapel Hill, NC: University of North Carolina Press, 1992.

Yueh, Linda. "A Quick Review of 250 Years of Economic Theory About Tariffs." *Harvard Business Review*, July 26, 2018. https://hbr.org/2018/07/a-quick-review-of-250-years-of-economic-theory-about-tariffs.

INDEX

ABOUT THE AUTHOR

Avery Elizabeth Hurt has written many history and science books for students of all ages. She particularly enjoys exploring the ways that the economic and social policies of the past play out in the present. With every book she writes, she is more impressed with how studying the past helps us understand the present—and how studying the present illuminates the past.